POLES APART

POLES APART

APART

ELAINE SCOTT

VIKING

To Parker, my polar opposite and my other half, with love

ACKNOWLEDGMENTS

Books begin as ideas, grow into outlines, and finally become the kind of book you hold in your hand. *Poles Apart* would not exist without the wonderful editorial work of Janet Pascal, who asked all the right questions and made all the right suggestions. It was a joy to work with her, and I want to thank her here.

Jim Hoover is the book's designer. He created the jacket and the drawings inside the book, and placed every photograph on every page. Somehow, he managed to make *Poles Apart* look warm and cool and beautiful—all at the same time. Thank you, Jim.

And to the explorers of old and the researchers of today, thank you for going to the ends of the Earth in order to help us understand this planet we call home.

VIKING
Published by Penguin Group
Penguin Young Readers Group, 345 Hudson Street, New York, New York 10014, U.S.A.
Penguin Books Ltd, 80 Strand, London WC2R 0RL, England
Penguin Books Australia Ltd, 250 Camberwell Road, Camberwell, Victoria 3124, Australia
Penguin Books Canada Ltd, 10 Alcorn Avenue, Toronto, Ontario, Canada M4V 3B2
Penguin Group (NZ), cnr Airborne and Rosedale Roads, Albany, Auckland 1310, New Zealand

First published in 2004 by Viking, a division of Penguin Young Readers Group

1 3 5 7 9 10 8 6 4 2

LIBRARY OF CONGRESS CATALOGING-IN-PUBLICATION DATA IS AVAILABLE.
ISBN 0-670-05925-0

Manufactured in China
Set in Zapf Humanist BT

PHOTO CREDITS
Frontispiece: George Holton/Photo Researchers, Inc.; Page 7: Jeffrey Kietzmann/National Science Foundation; Page 8: National Oceanic and Atmospheric Administration/Department of Commerce; Page 11: U.S. Department of the Interior, U.S. Geological Survey; Page 13: Steve Roof; Page 14: Map Resources; Pages 16, 17: graphics by Jim Hoover; Page 18: © Bjarne Riesto; Page 19, 42: Brien Barnett/National Science Foundation; Page 23: George Lepp/Getty Images; Page 24: B. Sidney/Getty Images; Page 25: Photodisc Collection/Getty Images; Page 27: NASA/GSFC/JPL, MISR Team; Page 28: Ferdinand Valk, Earth at Large; Page 29: © 1999 Rudy Brueggemann. All rights reserved; Page 31: Courtesy of the Thomas Fisher Rare Book Library, University of Toronto; Page 31: © Copyright Bryan & Cherry Alexander Photography; Page 32: Photodisc Collection; Page 33: Digital Vision/Getty Images; Page 34: National Oceanic and Atmospheric Administration/Department of Commerce; Page 35: Joseph Van Os/Getty Images; Page 36: Kristan Hutchison/National Science Foundation; Page 37: Jon Nickles/U.S. Fish and Wildlife Service; Page 38: Thomas D. Mangelsen/Images of Nature Stock Agency; Page 40: Paul Nicklen/Getty Images; Page 44: Treasures of the National Oceanic and Atmospheric Administration Library Collection; Page 45, 47, 49: © National Maritime Museum, London, Greenwich Hospital Collection; Page 51: National Oceanic and Atmospheric Administration/Department of Commerce; Page 52: Courtesy of the Thomas Fisher Rare Book Library, University of Toronto and Cook Collection, Frederick A. Cook Society; Page 55: Melanie Conner/National Science Foundation; Page 56: National Oceanic and Atmospheric Administration/Pacific Marine Environmental Laboratory; Page 57: Mark Sabbatini/National Science Foundation; Pages 58, 59: NASA; Page 60: Josh Landis/National Science Foundation; Page 61: Photograph by: Dr. Bill Servais/D.D.S. McMurdo Hospital/National Science Foundation.

✴ CONTENTS ✴

INTRODUCTION

Sunset over an iceberg near the South Pole. The beauty and mystery of the polar lands have intrigued scientists and adventurers for centuries.

IMAGINE THESE WORDS, written in a diary long ago, left open for others to find, read, and preserve. The year was 1912. The place was the Beardmore Glacier, high in the Transantarctic Mountains of Antarctica. The author was Captain Robert Falcon Scott of the British Royal Navy, who with his party, had set out for the South Pole. After a brutal seventy-eight-day trip that included skiing, sledging, walking, staggering, and stumbling through snow and ice, an entry in that diary brims with hope.

POLES APART

"It is wonderful to think that two long marches would land us at the Pole. We left our depot today, with nine days' provisions, so that it ought to be a certain thing now, and the only appalling possibility the sight of the Norwegian flag forestalling ours. . . . Only 27 miles from the Pole. We ought to do it now."

And then, on Thursday morning, January 18, 1912, after a terrible two-day trek through blizzards of snow and ice and temperatures that ranged from −22 to −23.5 degrees Fahrenheit, another entry reads, "We have just arrived at this tent, two miles from our camp, therefore 1½ miles from the Pole. In the tent we find a record of five Norwegians having been here as follows: Roald Amundsen, Olav Olavson Bjaaland,

Scott and his crew sailed from New Zealand to the Ross Sea aboard his ship Terra Nova, *which means "new land." Leaving the ship in the pack ice of the Ross Sea, the men still had an 800-mile trek to the South Pole.*

Hilmer Hanssen, Sverre H. Hassel, Oscar Wisting; 16 Dec. 1911." Scott's "appalling possibility" had taken place. The Norwegians had beaten him to the South Pole.

Before setting out on the return journey to the base camp, a despairing Scott wrote, "Great God, this is an awful place and terrible enough for us to have laboured to it without the reward of priority. . . . Now for the run home. . . . I wonder if we can do it."

Sadly, they could not. One by one, over dozens of terrible days, Edgar Evans, Titus Oates, Bill Wilson, Birdie Bowers, and Scott himself died. When rescuers found their frozen bodies, they also found Scott's diary. The last entry read, "We shall stick it out to the end, but we are getting weaker, of course, and the end cannot be far. It seems a pity, but I do not think I can write more. R. Scott." And in a final postscript, "For God's sake look after our people." When their bodies were found, the men were only eleven miles from their next food depot, and only a short run from home.

Though Scott's people perished with him, others still follow in their footsteps. Even today, hardship and the risk of death are a reality of life at the North and South Poles, the points at either end of Earth's axis that are so alike in some ways, and so different in others. However, today's risk-takers are more likely to be scientists than explorers. These engineers, astronomers, physicists, biologists, space scientists, physicians, construction workers, pilots, and mechanics are not seeking glory. Instead they are seeking answers.

Scientists at the poles have questions about such topics as Earth's magnetic field, the drift of its continents, and the changes in its climate. Why does winter come to the Arctic in December and to Antarctica in June? Why do polar bears live only in the Arctic and penguins only in Antarctica? Why did people settle in the Arctic but not in Antarctica? And why is the North Pole in the sea and the South Pole on land? Today we know the answers to these questions, but there are always others to take their place. Dedicated men and women search for answers to these questions, and many more, in these beautiful and mysterious lands that truly are poles apart.

1 DRIFTING APART
GONDWANALAND AND LAURASIA

THE NORTH AND SOUTH POLES—and the Arctic and Antarctica—have not always been the frozen places they are today. About 57 million years ago—long before any people lived on Earth—the sea and land that would become the Arctic and Antarctica were warm and tropical. In fact, all of Earth was still so warm that alligators lived on Ellesmere Island, which today is in the Arctic, close to the North Pole. And dinosaurs lived in Antarctica, which is now home to the South Pole! Scientists know this because they have found the fossils of dinosaurs, along with other tropical plants and creatures, buried deep beneath the polar ice of both places.

How can this be? The Arctic and Antarctica have not always been located where they are today. Long ago, they were much closer to the equator. They arrived in their present location through a process called continental drift.

A German scientist, Alfred Wegener, developed the theory of continental drift in 1915. When Earth was young, 200 million years ago, its land was not broken into the seven continents we know today. Instead, there was just one supercontinent, a huge mass of land near the equator that geologists have named Pangea, a Greek word meaning "all the land." Because Pangea was close to the equator, it was warm. Palm trees grew there. Alligators and dinosaurs roamed the land. But beneath its surface, Earth was on the move.

If you could slice our planet in half and look at its layers, you would see that its crust—the land on the surface—is only about 15 to 22 miles thick. Beneath the crust, there is another layer composed of thick plates of rock. These giant rock plates float on top of Earth's core, which is an 8,000-degree Fahrenheit liquid mass of molten and moving rock and metal.

Most of the time, you cannot feel the Earth move beneath your feet because the movement is so slight. These small movements are measured by scientific instruments called seismographs. Occasionally, however, the plates collide, and when the effects of that collision are strong enough to reach Earth's surface, it causes an earthquake.

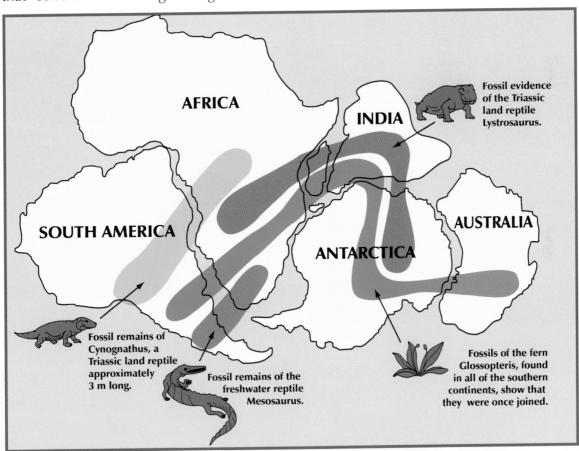

Alfred Wegener, who developed the theory of continental drift, realized that if the continents were fit back into each other, the locations of animal and plant fossils formed definite patterns across the continents. He compared the match to putting a torn page back together and being able to read across the lines.

POLES APART

Earthquakes seem sudden, but in fact, it takes a long time for the rock plates beneath Earth's crust to come together or break apart. One hundred fifty million years ago, Pangea began to break into two smaller continents, which scientists later named Laurasia and Gondwanaland. As ages passed, and Earth continued to move, Laurasia and Gondwanaland eventually broke into the seven continents we know today—Africa, Antarctica, Asia, Australia, Europe, North America, and South America.

Did you notice that the Arctic is missing from that list? That is because the Arctic is not a continent. It is a frozen sea, surrounded by the frozen edges of many different lands that belong to many different countries. Today, the lands that edge the Arctic Sea belong to the United States, Canada, Greenland (Denmark), Iceland, Norway, Sweden, Finland, and Russia. Antarctica, on the other hand, is a continent—a mass of land surrounded by icy seas.

So how did the fossils of tropical plants and creatures wind up near the North and South Poles? Fossils are the remains of ancient animals or plants that become embedded in the earth's rocks and soil. When Laurasia was part of tropical Pangea, plants and animals lived there. Their remains formed fossils after they died. As Laurasia slowly broke away from Pangea and began its drift to the north, it carried fossils of tropical creatures deep within its soil. Later, when the world slipped into its first Ice Age, the fossil remains of dinosaurs, alligators, and primitive palm trees were preserved, buried under layers of Arctic ice that is millions of years old.

Antarctica was once part of Gondwanaland. Like Laurasia, Gondwanaland was warm, and prehistoric tropical creatures such as dinosaurs lived there, too. Eventually a large mass of land broke away from Gondwanaland and began to drift south. Part of that land became the continent we know as Australia. More time passed, and about 45 million years ago, a mass of land broke away from Australia and began to drift even farther south, carrying its tropical fossils with it. Today, we call that continent Antarctica. When the first Ice Age buried Earth in glaciers, Antarctica's tropical fossils were buried and preserved beneath layers of ice that are also millions of years old.

When Laurasia broke up, its landmasses stayed connected by a land bridge between North America and Asia, close to what is now Russia and Alaska. But Antarctica had no land bridge connecting it to another continent. It was isolated—a huge frozen land at the bottom of the world, surrounded by treacherous seas. Antarctica's northernmost peninsula is separated from the southern tip of South America by the Drake Passage—a 400-mile-wide stretch of the fiercest, most dangerous waters in the world.

Antarctica is Earth's coldest continent. The world's record low temperature—129 degrees Fahrenheit below zero—was measured here.

Antarctica is Earth's highest continent, too. Because it is so mountainous, its average

*Scientists called paleontologists discovered these fossils of leaves
that had been buried beneath the Antarctic ice for millions of years.*

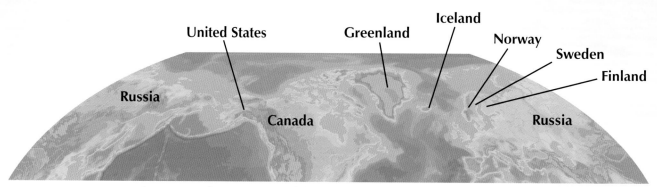

Russia — United States — Canada — Greenland — Iceland — Norway — Sweden — Finland — Russia

The Arctic is a frozen sea surrounded by land belonging to many different countries.

elevation is 8,200 feet. Its tallest mountain, Vinson Massif, rises to 16,062 feet. By comparison, Asia, the continent containing the mighty Himalayan Mountains, has an average elevation of only 2,900 feet, even though it is home to the world's highest mountain, Mount Everest, which is 29,035 feet.

And Antarctica is also Earth's windiest continent. During the Antarctic winter, the Katabatic winds blow counterclockwise at speeds of over 200 miles per hour, racing down from the mountains in Antarctica's interior to its coast. Antarctica is the coldest, highest, windiest place on Earth. And for most of history, no one even knew it existed.

Antarctica is frozen land, the fifth largest continent in the world.

2 POLES APART
SUMMER AND WINTER

PEOPLE OFTEN REFER to the North Pole as the "top" of the world, and the South Pole as the "bottom." Perhaps that is because on flat maps, north is always shown at the top, and south is at the bottom. However, since Earth is a sphere, of course there really isn't a top or bottom to it. There is another, more accurate way to talk about the poles and where they are located—their latitudes.

Earth is divided into its northern and southern hemispheres by an imaginary line running east and west that circles Earth at its middle—the equator. Latitudes are a series of imaginary parallel lines that circle Earth north and south of the equator, measuring distance in degrees from that middle point, which is zero. Like any circle, Earth has 360 degrees. So if you measured from the equator to the North Pole, which is one-quarter of the way around the world, you would have come 90 degrees. And if you measured from the equator to the South Pole, you would also travel one-quarter of the way around the world, also 90 degrees. To differentiate between the two 90-degree latitudes, the global address of the North Pole is 90 degrees north, and the global address of the South Pole is 90 degrees south, or –90 degrees.

Most places also have "east" or "west" in their address. Longitude lines divide the earth into "east" and "west" and are measured from zero at the Prime Meridian in Greenwich, England. Unlike latitude lines, longitude lines are not parallel. The poles have no longitude number, because east and west come together at the poles, where all the longitude lines meet. If you stand exactly at the North Pole, you will always face south, even if you turn around in a complete circle. And if you stand exactly at the South Pole, you will always face north. At the poles, there is no east or west.

So now you know exactly where the geographic North and South Poles are located. But what is a pole?

Earth rotates on its axis, another imaginary line, one that runs through the center of the planet and extends outward through its crust. If you look at a globe of the earth, you will notice that it isn't exactly straight in its stand. It's tilted on the metal rod around which it spins—its axis. Globes

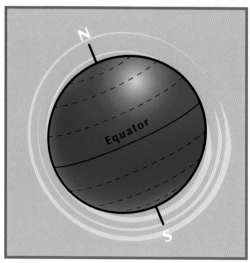

The equator is an imaginary line that circles the earth, dividing the globe into north and south.

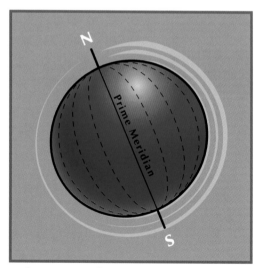

The Prime Meridian is another imaginary line, which goes from the North Pole to the South Pole. It divides the earth into east and west.

are made that way because Earth's axis is tilted that way—about 23.5 degrees to be exact. The North and South Poles mark the spot where the axis would meet Earth's surface at its northern and southern points—if the axis weren't an imaginary line.

If you extend the line of the axis out beyond the Earth's surface, it indicates two spots in the sky called the celestial poles. From ancient times, navigators have studied the stars to help them find their way across the seas and over strange lands. You can use the constellations to find the celestial poles in the night sky. The Big Dipper is made up of seven bright stars. It rotates around Polaris, the North Star, which is the star closest to the celestial North Pole. The two stars at the end of the bowl of the Big Dipper are called "pointer stars," because you can draw an imaginary line through them, and they will always point to Polaris, so you can always find north. Before the Civil War, escaping slaves in America called the constellation the Drinking Gourd and used it as a signpost in the sky that pointed north, toward freedom. There is no star in the Southern Hemisphere that is close enough to the celestial South Pole to be useful in navigation. But a constellation called the Southern Cross points toward it.

Earth spins around its axis, a little like the way a top spins around the pole that runs through its center, wobbling and leaning a bit as it goes. As it spins on its axis, Earth marks off time. One spin takes 24 hours—a single day. It takes 365 days—a full year—for Earth to make one orbit around the sun. During the year, most places on Earth experience four seasons—spring, summer, autumn, and winter. However, no matter what the season, most of the world gets some sunlight every day. But that is not so at the poles. At the poles, there are only two seasons—summer and winter.

Earth's seasons are caused by the tilt of Earth's axis. Summer officially comes to the Northern Hemisphere around June 21. This is the summer solstice, the longest day of the year. On the solstice, the northern end of Earth's axis,

Alaska's state flag clearly shows how the Big Dipper points to Polaris, although actually Polaris is slightly further away than the flag indicates.

Parts of the Arctic burst into bloom in summer. Throughout the year, the Arctic is warmer than Antarctica, because the Arctic Ocean absorbs the heat from the sun.

the pole, is tilted as far as it gets toward the sun. On that day, the Northern Hemisphere receives more hours of direct sunlight than any other day of the year. The hours of sunlight and darkness are evenly divided at the equator, but moving north from the equator, the days of summer become longer at every latitude. At 66.5 degrees north you reach "the land of the midnight sun." In all the lands above this line—which is called the Arctic Circle—on the actual day of the solstice, the sun doesn't set at all. At each latitude above the Arctic Circle, there are more and more days when the sun doesn't set, until finally, at the North Pole, the day doesn't end, and the sun never sets at all for six whole months. It just makes a 360-degree circle in the sky above.

On June 21 in the Southern Hemisphere, things are just the opposite. The South Pole is tilted away from the sun. Beginning at the equator and moving south, the days become shorter and shorter, until at 66.5 degrees south, you reach the Antarctic Circle, where on the day of the solstice the sun does not rise at all. Finally, as you reach the South Pole, the sun dips below the horizon for good and the land is plunged into darkness that will last until Earth has reached the other side of the sun six months later, and the entire process is reversed.

The sun disappears from the North Pole for six months on the first day of fall—the autumn equinox—around September 23. It will not reappear until the first day of spring—the vernal equinox—around March 21. On December 21, the day of the winter solstice, the sun will not rise anywhere above the Arctic Circle. Of course, while the Arctic is experiencing its long dark season, Antarctica is having its long season of sunlight. And then, as the Arctic emerges from the darkness on the first day of spring, Antarctica will plunge into it again, enduring a far harsher winter than anywhere else in the world.

Antarctica, the only continent with no native inhabitants, is governed by the Antarctic Treaty signed December 1, 1959, by Argentina, Australia, Belgium, Chile, France, Japan, New Zealand, Norway, South Africa, the U.S.S.R., the United Kingdom, and the U.S.A. Other countries joined to create the agreement in effect today. At McMurdo Station, a bust of American explorer Richard E. Byrd is surrounded by flags from the nations that have signed the Antarctic Treaty.

3 MUTUAL ATTRACTION
THE MAGNETIC POLES

HAVE YOU EVER WONDERED WHY the needle in a compass always swings toward the north? The answer is magnetism. A compass needle is itself a magnet, and it is reacting to the magnetic forces exerted by the earth.

Every magnet has two poles—a north pole and a south pole. Sometimes these poles are called "positive" and "negative." The north pole of one magnet will be attracted to the south pole of another, which is proba-bly where the expression "opposites attract" comes

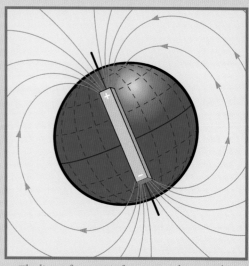

The lines of magnetic force come close together at a magnet's poles, which is why magnetism is strongest at the poles.

from. An invisible force called a magnetic field surrounds all magnets and causes this attrac-tion—magnetism. The magnetic field is strongest closer to the magnet, and gets weaker—though it still exists—as its distance from the magnet increases.

In 1600, an English scientist named William Gilbert developed the theory that the earth itself is a gigantic magnet. Later, scientific discoveries proved that Gilbert was correct. The earth is a gigantic magnet, and like every other magnet, it has two magnetic poles—the magnetic North Pole, and the magnetic South Pole.

Because the compass needle is a magnet too, one end is attracted to Earth's magnetic North Pole, while the other end is attracted to the South Pole, so the needle will always be pulled to point north. If you have ever used a compass, you may have noticed that its needle seems to "float" on top of a pin inside the case. Usually, as the needle turns to indicate a direction, it stays in a horizontal position. However, if you were approaching either the north or south magnetic pole, you would see that needle begin to tip downward. If there were enough room in the case, and if the needle could move freely, it would tip all the way down, until it pointed straight at the pole.

Unlike the North and South geographic Poles—whose latitudes are always exactly 90 degrees north and 90 degrees south—Earth's magnetic poles tend to wander a bit (about 10 to 15 miles a year) thanks to complicated changes in the layers of atmosphere above the earth, and the movement of the melted iron core inside. However, despite their wanderings, the magnetic North Pole is always in the Arctic, and the magnetic South Pole is always in Antarctica. Both magnetic poles are close to their corresponding geographic ones, but the compass needle points to the magnetic pole, not the geographic one.

There are two basic kinds of magnets—bar magnets and electromagnets. Earth is more like an electromagnet than a bar magnet. Electromagnets are created when electricity moves around metal. At the very center of Earth there is a metal core made of iron and nickel. The outer layers of that core are so hot they are molten, or melted. This is where Earth's magnetism begins. As the earth rotates, the soft metal layer swirls around the solid inner core. The swirling movement creates massive electrical currents that are hundreds of miles wide. The currents flow through the core at thousands of miles an hour, and as they move, they create Earth's magnetic field.

Earth's magnetic power is focused at its magnetic north and magnetic south poles, but it doesn't stay there. It travels outward, passing through the layers of our planet, eventually moving through Earth's crust and even extending outward into space. Scientists call the area where Earth's magnetic field extends into space the magnetosphere. The magnetosphere forms a protective shell around the earth, shielding it from the danger of the sun's solar wind. Solar wind is not like the wind that blows on Earth. It is actually a gas from the sun, called plasma, that is full of electrically charged particles called protons and electrons. Solar wind moves through the solar system at about a million miles per hour, and if it were to bombard Earth, it would singe our atmosphere until, over time, we would have no atmosphere left! With no atmosphere, the surface of Earth would look very different from what it does now, maybe like the surface of Mars. And life would not be possible on Earth. Scientists at NASA believe that Mars, which has little or no magnetosphere to protect it, lost most of its ancient oceans and its atmosphere because of the effects of solar wind. It's a very good thing Earth has a magnetosphere to protect it.

Even with a magnetosphere to protect the planet, sudden gusts in the solar wind can cause disturbances called space plasma storms. These solar storms often cause communication and science satellites to fail; they can even damage electric power systems on Earth. In 1989, one of these storms disrupted the Hydro-Quebec power system, and 6 million people in Canada and the United States were without electric power for over nine hours.

But this same solar wind also provides visitors to the Arctic and Antarctica with a spectacular polar light show—the aurora borealis and the aurora australis, also called the northern and southern lights. Of course, these are not "lights" the way we usually think of a light. The great streaks of color in the sky are caused when particles from the sun's solar wind enter Earth's atmosphere and collide with the oxygen and nitrogen that is

The aurora borealis inspired legends among the ancient people who saw it but could not explain it.

Perhaps Ezekiel's "gleaming amber" aurora looked something like this one.

present in it. When this collision happens, some of the particles' energy is changed into a kind of plasma-like light—the auroras. Scientists at the poles study the auroras because they are trying to learn more about the solar winds, Earth's atmosphere, and all the different ways Earth and the sun are connected to each other.

Today, science can explain what is going on as these lights dance over the ends of the earth, bathing it in spectacular and eerie bands of color, but how mysterious they must have looked to the ancient people who saw them. People living in the northern latitudes saw auroras frequently, and many superstitions and myths were created to explain them. The ancient people of the Arctic believed if you whistled at an aurora, it would sweep down and take you away. But they also believed that you could chase an aurora away by clapping your hands. The ancient Chinese based some of their early dragon legends on sightings of an aurora—its light resembling the flashing tail and fiery tongue of a dragon. And the ancient Scandinavians believed the auroras had the power to resolve conflicts and frequently painted aurora symbols on their war drums.

In a photograph taken from space, the aurora australis bathes the South Pole in spectacular green light.

People living nearer the equator are much less likely to see an aurora, although it does happen. Scholars believe the most ancient description of an aurora is found in the Old Testament of the Bible and describes one seen in Israel. In the sixth century B.C., the prophet Ezekiel wrote, "As I looked, a stormy wind came out of the north: a great cloud with brightness around it and fire flashing forth continually, and in the middle of the fire, something like gleaming amber."

For Ezekiel, the aurora was a vision from God. Though science today can tell us what causes an aurora, the sight of one in the night sky still produces wonder for those fortunate enough to see it.

4 THE PEOPLE
INUIT AND NONE

THE ARCTIC AND ANTARCTICA drifted to their current locations long before humans lived on this planet. Most scientists agree that humanity's earliest ancestors first appeared in Africa around 500,000 years ago. They remained there for hundreds of thousands of years, evolving and changing. And then they started to move. Earth's climate was changing, too, and anthropologists think the first wave of human migration left Africa in search of new food supplies around 60,000 years ago. During this migration, humans populated the southern coasts of India and Eurasia, eventually reaching Australia 50,000 years ago.

Thirty-five thousand years ago there was another migration. This time, our ancestors were hunting the animals that populated the grassy central Eurasian plains, or steppes. Eventually, some of these early hunters traveled west and populated Europe. Another group traveled east, populating East Asia, then moved north toward what is now Siberia. It is these people who were the first to see the northern lights, the aurora borealis. They were the ancestors of the Inuit, the native people of the Arctic.

Around 15,000 to 20,000 years ago, a small group of those Inuit ancestors began the first of several migrations across the land bridge that once connected Asia to North America. Today, we call that watery passage between Siberia and Alaska the Bering Strait. Even after the land bridge became submerged under water, the Inuit continued to migrate, crossing the strait in skin-covered boats they called kayaks. They traveled east from Siberia and eventually covered the coastal Arctic area all the way to eastern Greenland.

The people who migrated toward the northeast found they were living in a much colder climate than those who remained in Africa, or even Europe. Over time, they had to learn how to fish in the icy waters. Like their relatives who lived in warmer climates, they learned to make weapons crafted from animals' bones, antlers, horns, and teeth. The ancient Inuit used their weapons to hunt marine mammals such as seals, whales, and walrus. On land, they hunted caribou, polar bears, and smaller animals. They used the animals' skins to fashion warm fur parkas. They lived in skin-covered tents during the Arctic summer, and built sod houses to live in during the winter. Igloos built from blocks of ice

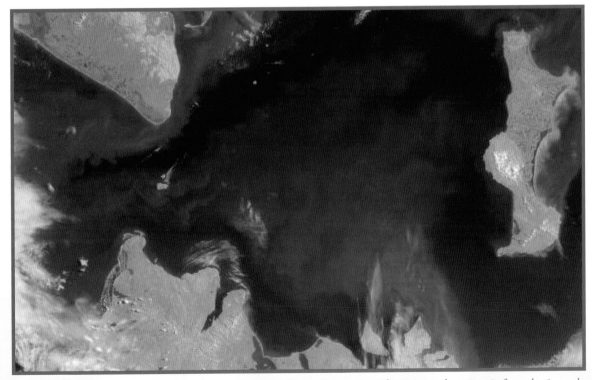

Shown from space, the watery passage known as the Bering Strait separates Siberia in northern Russia from the Seward Peninsula of Alaska in the United States. The distance across the strait is approximately 55 miles. North is to the left.

The Inuit developed unique means of transporting people and supplies over the Arctic snow and ice. Sledges pulled by dog teams have changed remarkably little over the centuries.

were just temporary dwellings, constructed during winter hunting trips. By 2500 B.C., using sleds to carry their belongings over the ice, the Inuit had settled across the entire Arctic, and all this time, no one else knew they were there.

Around a thousand years ago, the Vikings came to the Arctic. The first was Leif Erickson's father, Eric the Red. According to "The Saga of Eric the Red"—an oral history that was finally written down around 1200 A.D.—Eric the Red was banished from his native Norway to Iceland for killing a man. After he killed another man, he was banished from Iceland for three years. As part of the punishment, any person who found him remaining in Iceland was allowed to kill him! Eric the Red knew better than to stay, so he sailed west, looking for a new land. Near the North Pole, he found an island, the largest in the world.

Eric the Red named the island Greenland. He had a reason for calling this icy place by such a deceptively pleasant name. A man named Ari the Learned, who lived from 1067 to 1148 A.D., told the story of how Greenland got its name in his history, *The Book of the*

Icelanders. According to Ari the Learned, Eric the Red "named the country Greenland, and said it would make people want to go there if the country had a good name."

Greenland is not green. It sits where the Atlantic Ocean meets the Arctic Sea, not far from the North Pole. Eighty-five percent of it is covered with ice. However Earth's climate is constantly changing—gradually warming up and cooling down in cycles hundreds of years long. When Eric the Red left Iceland in search of Greenland, the Earth was in a warming trend, and climatologists—scientists who study weather patterns—believe the ice in the waters between Iceland and Greenland had almost disappeared. Therefore, the southern part of Greenland, while still quite cold, may indeed have been green for a little while during its short summer.

Naming the frozen island Greenland in order to attract settlers apparently worked, because in 986 A.D., twenty-four boatloads of Viking settlers set out from Iceland to settle there. Only fourteen boats made the trip successfully, but those people settled in the

The remains of Eric the Red's settlement in Greenland remind visitors of the Vikings' presence in North America.

POLES APART

Arctic five hundred years before Columbus discovered America.

In Greenland, Eric the Red discovered ancient Inuit settlements. According to Ari the Learned, "There, both in the East and the West, they found human habitations and fragments of skin boats and stone implements, from which it was evident that the same kind of people had been there as lived in Wineland and whom the Greenlanders called Skraelingjar." Wineland was an earlier Viking settlement. Its actual location is uncertain, but it was somewhere in Canada, south of Greenland, and it got its name because the Vikings made wine from the wild grapes that grew there.

Eventually, European Vikings in Greenland met the native people of the Arctic. There is archeological evidence that they traded together. Archeologists have found arrowheads made of metal, rather than the traditional stone, among the ruins of Inuit villages and have concluded that the Inuit learned about using metal from the Vikings. Unfortunately, the Vikings did not learn from the Inuit, who knew the best way to live in the Arctic. When the Vikings arrived in Greenland, they did not copy the Inuit way of life. Instead, they over-grazed the land and chopped down too many trees. And then the weather changed again.

Greenland turned colder. Indeed, the entire Arctic region became much colder. The ice crept further and further south, the seas froze, and ships loaded with supplies could no longer sail from Norway to Greenland. Historians think the Vikings and the Inuit began to fight over the dwindling supply of food, as animals could no longer graze on the frozen land. The Vikings lived in Greenland for about five hundred years, then gradually disappeared. Only the Thule, an Inuit tribe who are ancestors to today's Greenlanders, remained.

While the Inuit, and then the Vikings, settled in the Arctic, there were no people at all in Antarctica. No one even knew about the icy continent at the other end of the world, although the ancient Greeks thought it might be there. Aristotle (384-322 B.C.), the great Greek teacher and philosopher, understood that the world was round, and he taught that fact. The Greeks knew about the land in the north. They called it "Arktos," which means "The Big Bear,"

The word "Inuit" means "the people." Sometimes the Inuit are called Eskimos, but that is an American Indian word that means "meat eater," and is not one they use to describe themselves. Today many Inuit families use a snowmobile instead of a dogsled.

after the constellation above the North Pole that points to Polaris, the North Star.

The Greeks loved things to be balanced. North and south; right and left; good and bad; top and bottom—they liked to think in this way. Since the ancient Greeks knew that Arktos was at the top of the world, they reasoned that, for balance, there should be a land at the bottom of the world, too. They even gave this land a name—Antarkticos, which means "opposite the Arctic." For centuries, there was no proof that it existed anywhere but in the human imagination. No one had seen it, and no one had ever set foot on it.

Antarctica had drifted to its position at the bottom of the world, where it lay buried in the ice from the first Ice Age, long before there were any human beings on Earth. By the time humans finally began their migrations around the planet, Antarctica was already a frozen, isolated place, surrounded by treacherous seas. It was beyond any human reach.

Animals, however, were a different story.

5 NEVER NEIGHBORS
PENGUINS IN THE SOUTH

DESPITE THE FACT that Santa Claus is often pictured at the North Pole with penguins parading around him, nothing could be more incorrect. Of the seventeen species of penguins that live in today's world, not one of them has ever lived in the Northern Hemisphere, much less at the North Pole. Penguins belong to the Southern Hemisphere.

Today, the northernmost colony of penguins is located in the Galapagos Islands. These islands are close to the equator and 5,200 miles from the South Pole, though they do not look like typical tropical islands, and they do not have a warm tropical climate. The Humbolt Current, a flow of frigid water that runs from Antarctica through the Pacific Ocean and rises to the surface along the coasts of Chile and Peru, cools things down sufficiently to allow the Humbolt penguins to live there.

There are penguins in South Africa, too.

Adelie penguins are the smallest penguins in Antarctica. Adults are 2 feet tall and weigh 8 or 9 pounds.

Australia has colonies of penguins on its southern—and therefore, coldest—coast, and New Zealand, which is farther south still, is dotted with colonies of these interesting creatures. Six breeds of penguins live the farthest south, around the edges of Antarctica.

Scientists think the ancestors of today's penguins began their life when Laurasia and Gondwanaland were breaking away from Pangea, 140 million to 65 million years ago. During their time in Gondwanaland, the penguins' ancestors had lots to worry about. Many animals wanted to eat them—and they did. Penguins were dinner for dinosaurs, alligators, and dozens of other tropical creatures. However, most biologists believe the penguins' ancestors could fly, and so they could escape. When Gondwanaland began to break up, and the piece of land that became Antarctica started to drift to the south, it carried some of the penguins and other tropical creatures along with it.

Millions of years passed. The land moved farther and farther south, and the world turned colder and colder. The dinosaurs became extinct. Alligators and other tropical life that could not adapt to such a cold climate also disappeared from that part of the world. But in Antarctica, the penguins survived, because they were able to change.

Life in frozen Antarctica was certainly different from life in tropical Gondwanaland, and the penguin species evolved to adjust to that change, through a process that scientists call adaptation. Over time, the ancestors of today's penguins began to adapt to their chilly new home. Since there were no animals left to eat them, they had no need to fly. Their bodies began to change. Their wings grew smaller—way too small to lift them into the air, but

Emperor penguins are the largest penguins in the world. They can grow to almost 4 feet and weigh as much as 88 pounds.

not too small to propel them deep into the icy Antarctic seas. There they dined on small fish and tiny shrimplike creatures called krill, and learned to watch out for new enemies—killer whales and seals.

In order to stay warm in Antarctic temperatures that can drop to less than −100 degrees Fahrenheit, the penguins changed in other ways, too. Today their bodies are insulated with a thick coat of feathers—about seventy-five for every square inch—that are laid on top of each other like shingles on a roof. Beneath those feathers, there is another layer of soft feathers called down, and a layer of blubber, or fat. The penguins' outer feathers are oily, which makes them waterproof. Together, the feathers and fat provide a nice, warm coat that protects penguins from ice, snow, and the chill of frequent dives into a frigid Antarctic sea.

Penguins live on the land—but only in the coastal areas. No creatures live inland on Antarctica. It is simply too cold and too windy for them to survive. Penguins are very social

This picture of diving penguins appeared in 1913 in the journals of Scott's ill-fated final expedition. A penguin can dive down as much as nine hundred feet. Though penguins are easily visible when parading on the white ice, their coloring makes them hard to see when they dive into Antarctica's icy seas hunting for fish.

A group of Emperor penguin chicks. Emperor penguins do not build nests for their eggs.
Instead, males incubate the single egg on their feet for sixty-five days.

animals. They live together in colonies, and huddle next to each other to provide warmth. Huddling is a form of adaptation to life in a frigid land. Their chicks are raised together in a group called a "crèche." There may be hundreds of penguin chicks in one crèche, but each of them is fed by its own parents. A penguin chick recognizes its parents by the sound of their call.

Penguins got their name from another wingless bird, one that lived in the Northern Hemisphere, close to the Arctic—the Great Auk. As it adapted to the cold climate, the Great Auk had also lost its ability to fly, and learned to dive into icy seas for food. European explorers called the Great Auk a "penguin," which means "pin wings." Later, when they saw similar-looking wingless birds in Antarctica, they called them "penguins," too.

Since penguins are not afraid of humans, it is easy for scientists to get close to penguins as they do their research.

Penguins have been more fortunate than the Great Auks of the Arctic. Polar bears—and human beings—hunted the Arctic birds, and in 1844, the last Great Auk was killed. The species is now extinct.

That will not happen to the penguins. Since there are no polar bears, or any other predatory animals, on the land in Antarctica, penguins have no enemies. People are not allowed to hunt there, so penguins have learned not to be afraid of humans. People who visit Antarctica are able to walk right up to a colony of penguins, and these birds will not waddle away.

Some folks have wondered if penguins could be transplanted to the Arctic and survive there. The answer is, probably not. Penguins need certain kinds of food and certain kinds of terrain in order to feed and breed. And their trusting natures would make them very vulnerable to all of the wildlife that lives on the Arctic tundra. A polar bear, a wolf, or any other Arctic animal would have little trouble catching penguins for dinner. No animals from the Arctic have ever been taken to Antarctica, and it's best for the penguins if they appear at the North Pole only on Christmas cards!

6 NEVER NEIGHBORS
POLAR BEARS IN THE NORTH

MOST SCIENTISTS BELIEVE the ancestors of today's white polar bears were once brown bears—grizzlies—that lived in Siberia, in northern Russia, back when Russia was part of Laurasia. Like the penguins when they drifted south, the brown bears, when they drifted north, needed to adapt to a new life in a new place or die.

During the Ice Age around 100,000 years ago, scientists think the huge glaciers that formed in northern parts of Russia isolated a large pack of brown grizzly bears. Forced to live in a white world of ice and snow in order to survive, these grizzlies—like the penguins—adapted to their new environment. And because they adapted, they survived.

Today's polar bears are very different from the grizzly bear, which is now a distant relative.

Polar bears may look cuddly, but they are not. They are the largest meat-eating animals on Earth, and adult males can weigh 2,000 pounds.

The adaptation of the grizzly bears took thousands of years to complete. Eventually, their fur turned from brown to a creamy white. White fur allowed the bears to blend into their world of ice and snow, making it more difficult for the Inuit, who hunted them, to see their prey. The bear's fur also developed a top layer of guard hairs. Scientists believe these hollow hairs, which have no color, carry heat from the sun through the thick layer of fur and down to the polar bear's skin, helping to warm it. Beneath all that white fur, the polar bear has black skin—and a black tongue, too! The bears' black skin absorbs heat from the sun, which is another way polar bears have adapted to keep warm.

Over time, the shape of the bears' bodies changed, becoming longer and sleeker than their brown bear ancestors. Their necks grew longer, too. With its long neck and sleek body, a polar bear is built for swimming—and can it swim! Stretching its long neck upward to hold its head out of the water, a polar bear can swim as far as 60 miles without stopping. And if need be, a polar bear can swim underwater for two minutes—a long time for any creature, including a human, to hold its breath.

Their feet changed, too. The front paws grew large—almost 12 inches wide—and fur covered the soles. These wide, furry feet act as a kind of snowshoe and help the bears walk on the pack ice of the Arctic. In general, the Arctic is a much warmer place than Antarctica, because it is a frozen sea and not frozen land. However, Arctic winters can get down to an average temperature of –17 degrees Fahrenheit, which is very cold for hunting and fishing.

Because of its more hospitable climate, there are many more animals in the Arctic than in Antarctica. Fox, caribou, and musk ox roam the pack ice. Seals, walrus, and whales populate the sea—and the seals and walrus come to the edges of land. Ducks, geese, gulls, and terns are common there, and all of these creatures provide dinner for a hungry polar bear. A polar bear's favorite food is a seal, but it will eat just about anything that nature provides, including reindeer, walrus, fish, and even whales! However, if there is plenty of game, polar bears eat only the fat from the animals they kill. Their bodies can turn fat into energy more quickly than meat, so a well-fed polar bear will leave the meat for other scavenging animals. If times are lean, the polar bear will eat every scrap, and since these bears are the largest carnivores on Earth, no other Arctic animal challenges them.

Polar bears do not hibernate the way black and brown bears do. Male polar bears hunt and fish year round. However, if food is scarce, a male polar bear's heart rate may slow down in order to conserve energy even as it keeps walking, hunting for food. Some scientists call this state a "walking hibernation."

Female polar bears go into a den when they are expecting cubs. A female polar bear who is pregnant eats heavily in August and September. When she is satisfied, she builds her den deep inside a snow bank, enters it, and around November or December gives birth to her cubs. The new family remains in the den until March or April. Then it is time to take the cubs outside and begin to show them how to survive in their Arctic world.

Sometimes people have wondered what would happen if a polar bear were to be transplanted to Antarctica. It could probably survive the cold, and there would be plenty of penguins to eat, but most scientists think female polar bears would not be able to find a suitable burrow or den to raise their infant cubs. Antarctica's cold is far worse than anything the Arctic winter produces, and bear cubs—if they were born there—would have a hard time surviving to adulthood.

But polar bears will never come to Antarctica. The Antarctic Treaty has said, among many other things, that Antarctica's special environment must be preserved. In order to help protect that environment, the treaty states that no new species of animals should be brought to Antarctica. The continent should be left as nature created it. The people who wrote the treaty knew that it's best to leave penguins and polar bears exactly where nature put them—at opposite ends of the earth.

Most polar bear mothers give birth to two cubs, or occasionally three. The cubs stay with their mother for two years, learning how to hunt and fish, before they can live on their own.

7 GREAT RACES
FIRST TO SEE THEM

LONG AFTER THE INUIT came to the Arctic, an ancient Greek sailor became the first European to write about the frozen seas at the top of the world. In 330 B.C., Pytheas, who was a geographer as well as a sailor, set out on a journey from a Greek settlement in what is now Marseilles, in the south of France. Pytheas was looking

Early explorers had great difficulty moving their ships through the slush ice. Today, specially designed ships can easily cut a path through the ice, which quickly refreezes once the ship has passed.

for amber and bronze. He had heard these items were to be found on some islands in the North Atlantic that we now call Great Britain.

In a journal called a ship's log, which he named *On the Ocean*, Pytheas wrote about meeting the native people of Britain, who told him of another land to the northwest, a land where the sun shone all night long. Like all true explorers, Pytheas was curious. He wanted to see this mysterious land for himself. So he left Scotland and sailed northward for six days.

On his way, Pytheas saw creatures as big as his ship, swimming and blowing out sprays of water from holes in their backs. He described them in his ship's log and became the first person to write about whales. Finally, Pytheas saw land in the distance. He called it Thule, which means "the unknown" in Greek. It was so cold there the sea turned to ice. Pytheas recorded what he saw, saying he had entered "an ocean of slush ice and fog so thick one could not sail through." He went on to write that the water and slush ice "binds all together, and can be traveled neither on foot nor by boat."

Pytheas had come as far north as modern Greenland and Iceland. He had discovered the land at the top of the world, the land of the Inuit—the Arctic. But he never left his boat, and he never met the people.

About three hundred years later, sometime in the seventh century, a Polynesian explorer may have been the first person to see Antarctica. The ancient Polynesians were wonderful sailors and navigators who explored the vast Pacific Ocean in double-hulled canoes dug out from tree trunks. They lashed these two hulls together with braided strands of coconut fibers that were strong enough to withstand a stormy sea. They wove their sails from coconut leaves, and if there was no wind to carry them, they paddled. And they traveled far.

There is a legend from the island of Rarotonga, in the South Pacific, about a Polynesian explorer living in the seventh century named Ui-te-Rangiora. According to the story, he

The ancient Polynesians were seafaring people who used outrigger canoes like the one above. When traveling great distances, they added sails to the canoes. Their descendents still use outriggers today.

"sailed south to a place of bitter cold where white rock-like forms grew out of a frozen sea." This could be the first description of Antarctic icebergs. Ui-te-Rangiora's story is a legend, and while ancient legends often have truth in them, we cannot say for certain that he saw Antarctica or its icebergs. A long time would pass before anyone definitely saw the icy continent.

As we saw, the Greeks were the first to propose Antarctica's existence, as early as the fourth century B.C. When the great Greek libraries at Alexandria in Egypt were destroyed around 400 A.D., many of the Greeks' ideas were forgotten. A few books—and therefore, ideas—survived; however, few paid attention to those ideas during Europe's Dark Ages, a time when most people were not encouraged to read, travel, or think for themselves.

When the Renaissance began in Europe, around 1450, people became more interested in ancient ideas about art and science. They began to travel and meet other people from other cultures. By 1492, explorers like Columbus were ready to set sail for the New World—though there were still plenty of people around who worried that this world was flat, and Columbus would sail off its edge. With exploration came maps—and the maps of the day were influenced by those Greek ideas of a land at the bottom of the world. Even though no one had ever seen it, and few believed it really existed, the Terra Australis Incognita, Latin for "Unknown Southern Land," is drawn on many medieval and Renaissance maps.

More centuries passed, and still no one had seen it. Then, in 1767, a British astronomer and mapmaker named Alexander Dalrymple brought the idea up again. He believed that there really was a continent in the Southern Hemisphere, somewhere in the

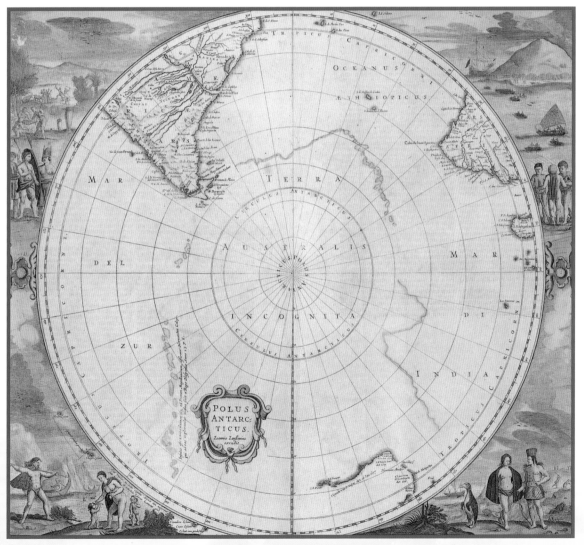

Old maps, such as this one published in 1638 in Jan Jansson's Novus Atlas, *clearly show the "Terra Australis Incognita" though at the time no one had ever been to Antarctica.*

Pacific Ocean south of what is now Tahiti. According to Dalrymple, his research told him this land was quite large. Though he had never seen the continent, Dalrymple wrote that it covered "a greater extent than the whole civilized part of Asia, from Turkey eastward to the extremity of China." Furthermore, Dalrymple was convinced this land was populated with at least fifty million people! He argued that the British government should look for the new continent and establish trade with the people living there, claiming that "the scraps from this table would be sufficient to maintain the power, dominion, and sovereignty of Britain by employing all its manufacturers and ships."

Dalrymple convinced the British government that this land existed. In turn, the British government commissioned Captain James Cook to undertake a voyage of exploration to find it. Cook, however, was not convinced it was there. Although Cook was always eager to explore, he did not think he would have a successful voyage, because he thought this Terra Australis Incognita was a myth.

Cook made three great ocean voyages, circling the globe in each one. His first voyage began in 1768, and during it he discovered the continent we call Australia. Then he sailed on, stopping for a while on the island of Tahiti, where he met Tupaia, another Polynesian explorer, like Ui-te-Rangiora over a thousand years earlier, who had vast knowledge of the South Pacific. Cook befriended Tupaia and took him aboard his ship, the *Endeavor*. Using Tupaia's knowledge, the *Endeavor* and her crew of eighty-five men sailed south, through the Drake Passage between the tip of South America and the top of the Antarctic Peninsula, but fog prevented them from seeing land. Cook returned to England in 1771 and declared that this voyage "must be allowed to have set aside most, if not all, arguments and proofs that have been advanced by different authors to prove that there must be a southern continent." In other words, Cook thought he had proved Antarctica did not exist.

But Dalrymple was not convinced, and the English sent Cook out a second time, as captain of the *Resolution*. His orders were to sail as far south as he could. Another ship, the *Adventure*, captained by Tobias Furneaux, sailed with him, but when the two ships

Captain James Cook (1728-1779) visited all seven continents in the course of his life. Because he did not set foot on the mainland, however, Cook refused to believe Antarctica existed. He was famous for insisting that his crews maintain personal cleanliness and eat fresh fruits and vegetables daily in order to prevent scurvy, a common disease of the time.

were separated in an Antarctic fog, the *Adventure* returned to New Zealand, and Cook sailed on alone.

On January 17, 1773, Cook became the first person to cross the Antarctic Circle. During this journey, he discovered South Georgia Island and the Sandwich Islands, and claimed them for King George III of England. But he still had not seen the mainland of Antarctica. Cook returned to England, certain that Antarctica did not exist. This time on his return, he said, "I had now made the circuit of the Southern Ocean in a high Latitude and traversed it in such a manner as to leave not the least room for the possibility of there being a continent, unless near the pole and out of the reach of navigation."

Captain James Cook was wrong.

8 GREAT RACES
FIRST TO CLAIM THEM

DESPITE COOK'S INSISTENCE that Antarctica did not exist, Alexander Dalrymple was convinced it was there. And he was a bit angry at the explorers who failed to find it. "The point is not yet determined whether there is or is not, a southern continent," he wrote. And then he could not resist adding this comment: "I would not have come back in Ignorance," adding the capital *I* in *ignorance* for emphasis.

By now, the idea of a southern continent was on everyone's mind. Four countries—England, France, Russia, and America—played important roles in its discovery. In the years that followed Cook's voyages, many explorers believed they had sighted Antarctica, but no one set foot on it until February 7, 1821, when the captain of an American whaling ship, John Davis, stepped on the continent for the first time. Since all explorers want to be the first to arrive at a new destination, some people argue that Davis did not actually walk on the continent itself, but only on the Antarctic Peninsula. A peninsula is a narrow body of land, almost surrounded on all sides by water. It is attached to its continent by a narrow strip of land. To most, stepping on the peninsula would seem to be the same thing as stepping onto the larger continent. But to those who want to be "first" the difference seemed important. If Davis's claim is rejected, the first confirmed landing on Antarctica was not until January 24, 1895, by the Norwegian Henryk John Bull.

Going to the Arctic and Antarctica has never been easy. People have attempted to travel there for various reasons—some went for adventure, some went for science, and still more went hoping to make money buying and selling goods. It was the desire for commercial gain that drove countries to sponsor expeditions through the icy Arctic area look-

ing for a "Northwest Passage" from Europe to Asia. Until such a passage was found, ships sailing from the Atlantic Ocean to the Pacific Ocean had to make the long voyage all the way south around the tip of Africa via the Cape of Good Hope, or South America via Cape Horn. Traveling through the waters of either of these capes was—and is—extremely dangerous.

One of the most tragic expeditions was that of British explorer Sir John Franklin. In 1845, he set off with 128 men in two ships—the *Erebus* and the aptly named *Terror*—in search of the Northwest Passage. Three years passed, and no one heard from the men. Search parties looked for them in vain. In 1856, Charles Dickens, along with another author, Wilkie Collins, wrote a play about Franklin's expedition called *The Frozen Deep*. Three years later, in 1859, a search party found the men's skeletons

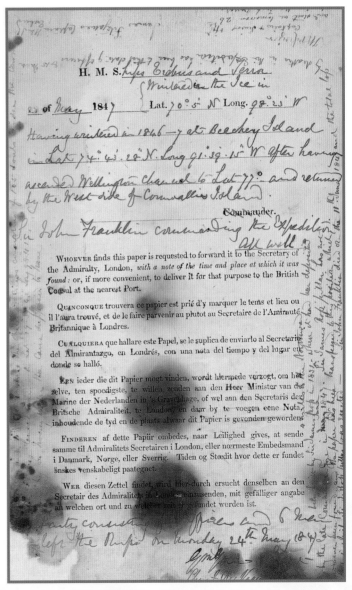

A page from the ill-fated Franklin expedition's journal is preserved at the National Maritime Museum in Greenwich, England.

and their diaries on the northwest coast of King William Island. The diaries, which had been placed inside a protective mound of stones called a cairn, gave their precise location. It was 74 degrees, 43 minutes, 28 seconds north, by 91 degrees, 39 minutes, 15 seconds west—just sixteen degrees or a little over 1000 miles from the North Pole.

One entry dated April 25, 1848 states, "The ships were frozen in the ice since 12th September. The officers and crew (105 men) are leaving the ships and starting back along the banks of the Fish river." The same entry goes on to say, "Sir John Franklin died on 11 June, 1847; and the total loss by deaths on the expedition so far has been to this date, nine officers and fifteen men." In truth, all 129 men of the Franklin expedition eventually died in the Arctic, as they searched for the Northwest Passage. So did many other explorers.

It was left to a Norwegian explorer, Roald Amundsen, to sail a single ship, the *Gjoa*, on the 900-mile passage through the icy Arctic islands of Canada, just 1,200 miles south of the North Pole. Amundsen began his westward journey in Greenland in the spring of 1903. When the Arctic winter set in, he allowed his boat to be frozen into the icy sea at a harbor that is now called Gjoa Haven.

While there, Amundsen became friendly with the Inuit people. Amundsen liked to call himself "the last of the Vikings," but unlike his Viking ancestors, he took the time to learn valuable survival skills from the Inuit. He learned how to build an igloo, how to wear fur parkas loosely to preserve body heat, and how to drive a sled pulled by a dog team. Years later, that would prove to be the most important lesson of all.

When the weather turned warmer, Amundsen and his crew forced the *Gjoa* from the softening ice. They sailed west, through uncharted waters, and then, on August 26, 1905, they saw a ship coming toward them from the opposite direction—traveling west to east. They had successfully navigated a northwest passage through the icy Arctic! Amundsen recorded these words in his diary describing the moment he saw the other ship and knew he had succeeded: "The North West Passage was done. My boyhood dream—at that

Roald Amundsen probably learned how to ski in his native Norway, but the Inuit taught him how to dress warmly in loose fur parkas.

moment it was accomplished. A strange feeling welled up in my throat; I was somewhat over-strained and worn—it was weakness in me—but I felt tears in my eye. 'Vessel in sight'. . . Vessel in sight."

The Northwest Passage interested explorers, but it was particularly important to traders who wanted to transport and sell their goods more easily. The North and South Poles, on the other hand, lured explorers and, later, scientists. Several organizations sponsored expeditions, and the race to the poles was on.

The North and South geographic Poles are very specific places on the earth—one is 90 degrees north latitude and the other is –90 degrees south. But neither pole stands out from the vast icy expanses that surround it. For those who got to the poles, there were no landmarks—no "X marks the spot" to let them know they had arrived. Early explorers had to rely on their calculations of latitude and longitude, and their compasses, to tell them where they were.

As explorers approached the poles, they paid close attention to their compasses. The nearer they got to the poles, the more the needle in the compass would try to point straight down. Their observations of their surroundings were important, too. Since all the expeditions tried to reach the poles in the summer, explorers checked the position of the sun. At the poles in the summer, the sun never sets. Instead, it makes a horizontal orbit in the sky. As they fought their way toward the poles, explorers kept detailed notes of all these strange things in their logbooks and journals. They would need this information to prove whether or not they had reached their goal.

A lack of detailed records prevented Dr. Frederick Cook from proving he had reached the North Pole.

The race to the North Pole was "won" in 1908 or 1909—depending on whose story you believe. The first person to claim this prize was an American, Dr. Frederick Cook, who said he reached the North Pole on April 12, 1908. Cook did not do a good enough job of recording his journey. Some people believe he actually faked his evidence, and later experts decided there was not enough in his logbooks to prove he had reached the North Pole. But not everyone agreed with this finding. There are still people today who think Cook was first.

Admiral Robert Peary was another American explorer who was obsessed with being the first to the North Pole. Before Cook returned from his 1908 trip to make his claim, Peary had already started on one of his many polar expeditions. Peary announced that on April 6, 1909, he had finally become the first man to reach the North Pole—after eighteen years of trying! Peary's expedition was well documented, but his personal claim is more controversial.

Matthew Henson, an African-American explorer, accompanied Peary on many of his journeys. The records of this expedition show that on April 6, 1909, Matthew Henson arrived at a place where his compass began to act in a strange fashion, the needle pointing down. The best reading he could get was 89 degrees, 47 minutes north latitude. The pole is 90 degrees north. Henson was very close; perhaps he was there. Had he read his compass slightly before he did, or slightly later, he might have seen it say 90 degrees. No one can stay still at the North Pole, because it is actually in the center of the Arctic Ocean. You can stand on this frozen ocean, but the ice pack will continue to move beneath you.

Henson had walked over the frozen sea, arriving at the pole forty-five minutes ahead of Admiral Peary, who was pulled on a sledge, a kind of sled used in polar exploration. On an earlier failed expedition, Peary had lost some toes to frostbite. At that time he said, "A few toes aren't much to give to achieve the Pole." But he didn't have many toes left, so it was sensible for him to travel on a sledge, even though it put him behind Matthew Henson.

When Peary's sled got pulled to the spot, Henson greeted him with the statement, "I think I am the first man to sit on top of the world."

According to Henson, Peary was "hopping mad." But it was Peary who on April 6, 1909,

Robert Peary and Matthew Henson worked together for years before they finally reached the North Pole.

planted a flag at 90 degrees north and declared, "Mine at last," claiming the victory for himself. Since it was obvious that Matthew Henson reached the pole before Peary, some historians say Henson did not receive the proper credit for being first, because of the racism of his day.

Norway's Roald Amundsen, who had already discovered the Northwest Passage, went on to become the first person to set foot at the South Pole. The lessons the Inuit had taught him about using dog sleds were crucial to Amundsen's success in this next adventure. He chose his sled dogs carefully, looking for animals that came from a long line of creatures that could survive the Arctic cold. He loved them and called them "our children." He knew their value and wrote, "The dogs are the most important thing for us. The whole outcome of the expedition depends on them." The dog teams did not let him down, and on December 14, 1911, Roald Amundsen raised Norway's flag at the South Pole and called the place Polheim, which means "Pole Home." No one has ever challenged Amundsen's claim to be first to the South Pole.

Since the North Pole is located in a frozen sea where the ice is always drifting, it has no marker. But the South Pole does—even though it has to be moved every year. It's not that the South Pole moves. It is always −90 degrees latitude. But the marker travels a bit. The South Pole is on land that lies frozen beneath the ice and snow of Antarctica. No one can reach the land—it is covered with a glacier, and glaciers move. The South Pole marker is nailed into a glacier that moves about 1.1 inches in a day. So every year, there is a ceremony to mark the "new" location of the South Pole.

But flags and markers are not the important things about the poles. Neither, really, is the question of who was first to reach them. The most important thing about the poles is that they were finally discovered and explored. Once that happened, research and learning could begin.

9 THE POLES TODAY
LESSONS FROM THE ICE

This new South Pole station will soon replace the Amundsen-Scott South Polar Station, affectionately called "The Dome." Note the jacks beneath the new station that will allow it to be raised as ice and snow accumulate around it.

THERE ARE MORE SCIENTISTS than explorers at the poles today. The Amundsen-Scott South Polar Station sits at the South Pole, where, during the Antarctic summer, approximately two hundred people work and do research. Around sixty people choose to remain there during the long polar winter. The station could be built right at the South Pole because the two-mile-thick sheet of ice has land beneath it, and the combination provides a firm foundation for a building.

Conditions are different at the North Pole. There is no permanent research station there, because the North Pole sits in the Arctic Ocean, on top of frozen ice. It isn't possible to construct a permanent building there. Instead, the North Pole is marked with cameras and instruments that send their information back to researchers in stations that are built on land within the Arctic Circle.

There are many different kinds of research going on at both poles. In the Arctic, scientists study the animal and plant life, the people, the climate and its effect on the rest of the world, and surprisingly, what it might be like to live on Mars! Devon Island, high in the Arctic Ocean, is home to this research project, which is called the NASA Haughton-Mars Project.

Because it is the site of a 23-million-year-old meteor crater, scientists believe that the

Only scientific instruments mark the location of the geographic North Pole. However from April to October, two solar powered Web cameras transmit images such as this one to the scientists at the National Oceanic and Atmospheric Administration (NOAA).

Two "Polies" relocate the marker for the geographic South Pole. From mid-February to late October, anyone who remains at the South Pole is isolated from the rest of the world.

dirt and rocks on Devon Island could be similar to those on Mars. They are studying the rocky terrain of Devon Island to try to learn more about how Mars came to be the kind of planet it is today. They have built a greenhouse there—the Arthur Clarke Mars Greenhouse named in honor of the man who wrote *2001: A Space Odyssey*—where they are experimenting with growing plants year-round in the Arctic, tending them during the long Arctic winter with automated systems. If human beings ever plan to inhabit Mars, they will have to know how to grow food in an unlikely environment, and Devon Island in the Arctic provides an excellent place to research and learn more about doing that.

At the South Pole, scientists study, among other things, the magnetosphere and the

In 1979, in this image seen from space, the polar ice cap covered much of the Arctic Sea. Greenland is the large snow-covered island on the right.

stars that lie beyond it; cosmic rays; the adaptation of marine and land animals to their icy environment; bubbles in the ice; and Lake Vostok, a 150-mile-long lake that lies beneath 2.4 miles of ice in East Antarctica.

Scientists estimate that Lake Vostok has been buried untouched beneath the ice for over 400,000 years. Researchers wonder what the icy water holds, and what a study of it would tell them. Some think the water may contain new life forms. Others say its sediments—solid materials that settled at the bottom—could contain a record of Earth's climate through the ages. So the science in Lake Vostok is new, exciting, and tricky. Right now, Lake Vostok is pristine. It has not had any contact with this world for 400,000 years. Any kind of research on its waters could contaminate them. Therefore, research is proceeding slowly, as everyone thinks about the best way to learn from the lake without harming it.

Another image from space, taken in 2003, shows how much the ice cap has melted.
The narrow water passage in the lower left corner of the picture is the Bering Strait.

Perhaps the research into global warming is the topic that interests everyone the most. Earth's temperature has not been steady over the millions of years of its existence. Today, average global temperatures are one degree Fahrenheit higher than they were one hundred years ago. That may not sound like much of an increase, but a few degrees can make a big difference. At the peak of the last ice age, about eighteen thousand years ago, glaciers covered most of North America. But the earth's average temperature was only around 7 degrees Fahrenheit less than it is today! So you can see that a small increase in temperature—7 degrees—can cause drastic changes to the world's climate.

People are concerned about the rise in Earth's temperature because it could affect all life on Earth. Even a little extra warming can cause problems for humans, animals, and plants. For example, a small increase in temperature can cause the ice at the poles to begin to melt. This could lead to widespread flooding. Food chains would be interrupted and life as we know it would change drastically.

The North Pole's ice floats on top of the Arctic Sea. If only the Arctic ice melted, scientists estimate that the sea level would rise about 20 to 23 feet, since the ice is already in the water. On the other hand, the South Pole's ice sits on land, and if it were to melt and run off into the ocean, the world's sea level would rise somewhere between 197 and 213 feet!

So scientists study Earth's climate, eager to understand whether our planet is warming up as part of its natural cycle of heating and cooling, or whether it is caused by something humans are doing to it—or a combination of both. For example, the Arctic has been in a warming trend throughout the 1990s, except for one year—1991—when the volcano Mount Pinatubo erupted in the Philippines. That volcano spewed ash and dust high in the atmosphere. Earth's atmosphere is sensitive to anything that is introduced to it, and scientists at NASA believe the particles in the atmosphere from Pinatubo caused a cooling in the Arctic. But the cooling was temporary. The Arctic is warming up again. Surface temperatures are increasing, melting the ice and causing water to pool on its surface.

Since water absorbs heat, while ice reflects it, the pools of water on the Arctic ice cap are absorbing heat. And that makes the ice cap melt even faster. The melted water also causes fractures in the ice cap. Eventually, entire shelves of ice can break away, and then smaller pieces of ice—icebergs—break off in an event called "calving." All of this activity puts more moisture into Earth's atmosphere, causing weather to change around the globe.

Scientists study the world's weather at the South Pole, too, trying to understand the weather patterns. They take

The Dome is in danger of being buried under Antarctica's snow and ice. The new station is seen in the background.

The moon setting over the mountains of Antarctica at sunrise on October 2. The sun will stay in the Antarctic sky until late February.

core samples from glaciers that have been on Earth for the past 160,000 years. They are able to study the air bubbles trapped in that ice, and from them they can tell what the Earth's climate was like thousands of years ago. They use that information to try to understand what Earth's climate may be like in the future. Earth may be in a warming trend, but the more we understand Earth and the way its systems work, the more we can do to protect it.

The "Polies"—people who stay at the South Pole year-round—live and work in the most remote part of Earth. In winter, the temperatures can plunge to –100 degrees Fahrenheit, or less. Going outside means putting on thirty-five pounds of clothing! It's not much better in the summer, when temperatures may rise to –30 degrees. Polies can communicate with their families around the world for ten hours a day, when the satellites pass above them. For the rest of the day, they are out of touch.

Working and learning in the Arctic and Antarctic is difficult and dangerous, but it is exciting and rewarding, too. The North and South Poles are unlike any other places on Earth. These remote regions are poles apart, but for the people who live and work at them, there is no place else they would rather be.

✳ INDEX ✳

Numbers in **boldface** refer to captions or illustrations.

✳ FURTHER READING ✳

Armstrong, Jennifer. *Shipwreck at the Bottom of the World: Shackleton's Amazing Voyage.* Crown Publications, 1998. Recreates Shackleton's harrowing journey.

Dwyer, Minday. *Aurora: A Tale of the Northern Lights.* Alaska Northwest Books, 2001. An original tale tells a "legend" of the colorful northern lights.

Flowers, Pam. *Big-Enough Anna: The Little Sled Dog Who Braved the Arctic.* Alaska Northwest Books, 2003. The true story of a determined dog who not only completes the 2,500 mile journey to the top of the earth, but also takes over when the lead dog is lost.

Harper, Kenn. *Give Me My Father's Body: The Life of Minik, the New York Eskimo.* Simon, 2001. Abridged for a young adult audience. Minik was one of six Greenland Inuits brought to the American Museum of Natural History by Robert Peary as living specimens in 1897.

Hooper, Meredith. *Antarctic Journal.* National Geographic, 2001. The author describes her summer at Palmer Station, an American science base.

Kimmel, Elizabeth Cody. *Ice Story: Shackleton's Lost Expedition.* Clarion Books, 1999. Follows the series of disasters that plagued the expedition.

McCurdy, Michel. *Trapped by the Ice!: Shackleton's Amazing Antarctic Adventure.* Walker, 2002. Through journals and Shackleton's own words, this riveting account brings his endurance and desperation to life.

McGonigal, David, and Dr. Lynn Woodworth. *Antarctica and the Arctic: The Complete Encyclopedia.* Firefly, 2001. A comprehensive guide to the polar regions with photographs, illustrations, maps, and more.

Miller, Debbie S. *Arctic Lights, Arctic Nights.* Walker, 2003. Follows the changing light and environmental attributes each month in an Arctic year.

Sabuda, Robert. *The Blizzard's Robe.* Atheneum, 1999. Batik art on paper illustrates this arctic pourquoi story that explains the origins of the northern lights.

——— WEBSITES OF INTEREST ———

Arctic National Wildlife Refuge
http://www.r7.fws.gov/nwr/arctic/wildlife.html

Arctic Theme Page
http://www.arctic.noaa.gov/gallery_np.html

Auroras: Paintings in the Sky
http://www.exploratorium.edu/learning_studio/auroras/

Bancroft Arnesen Expedition
http://www.yourexpedition.com/bae_archive/index.html

Canadian Arctic Profiles
http://collections.ic.gc.ca/arctic/english.htm

CIA—The World Factbook, Antarctica
http://www.cia.gov/cia/publications/factbook/geos/ay.html

Geomagnetism, Magnetic Fields, and the Magnetic North Pole
http://www.geolab.nrcan.gc.ca/geomag/home_e.shtml

Glacier
http://www.glacier.rice.edu/

The New South Polar Times
http://205.174.118.254/nspt/home.htm

Polar Bears International
http://www.polarbearsalive.org/

Smithsonian Arctic Studies Center
http://www.mnh.si.edu/arctic/index.html

South-Pole.com
http://www.south-pole.com/

State of Alaska on the Web
http://www.state.ak.us/kids/

Virtual Tour: Antarctica
http://astro.uchicago.edu/cara/vtour/

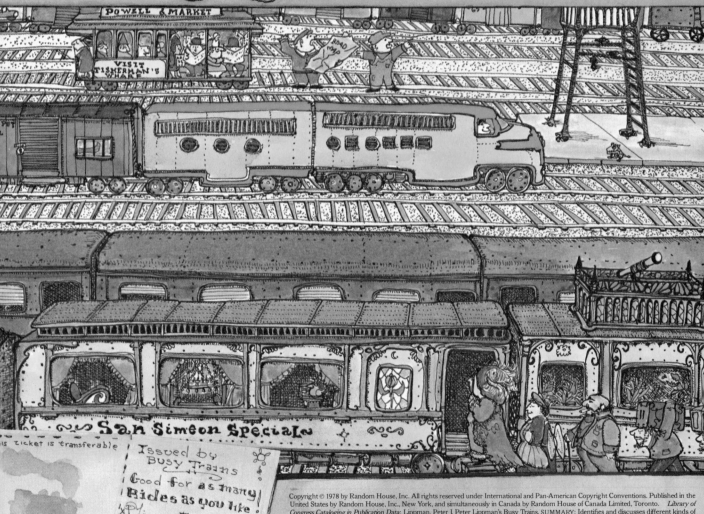

Busy Trains

RANDOM HOUSE 🏠 NEW YORK